A DVD-based
Study Guide

AFRICA
AND THE BIBLE

The Earliest Roots of the Faith

With Wintley Phipps

A DVD-based study series
Study Guide

AFRICA
AND THE BIBLE

The Earliest Roots of the Faith

With Wintley Phipps

Six Lessons for Group Exploration

DISCOVERY HOUSE

P U B L I S H E R S®

Feeding the Soul with the Word of God

The Daylight Bible Studies are based on programs produced by
Day of Discovery, **a Bible-teaching TV series of RBC Ministries.**

© 2013 by Discovery House Publishers

Discovery House Publishers is affiliated with RBC Ministries,
Grand Rapids, Michigan.

Requests for permission to quote from this book should be directed to:
Permissions Department
Discovery House Publishers
P.O. Box 3566
Grand Rapids, MI 49501
Or contact us by e-mail at permissionsdept@dhp.org

Study questions by Andrew Sloan
Interior design by Sherri L. Hoffman
Cover design by Jeremy Culp
Cover photo by iStockphoto

ISBN: 978-1-57293-781-9

Printed in the United States of America

First Printing 2013

CONTENTS

A New Understanding

Ignorance has been the root of so much trouble in our society. People who are not aware of valuable information often fill in the blanks with erroneous and sometimes harmful speculations. This is too often the case with the issue of racism and diversity in the church of Jesus Christ.

Long ago, incorrect interpretations of one tiny verse in the Old Testament began a thought process that was absolutely devastating to a group of people who have never deserved the treatment they received and sometimes still receive.

It is important that people on both sides of this situation begin to grasp the damage this interpretation has done, move to eliminate this erroneous thinking, and work harder to connect people on the basis of their faith and their shared humanity instead of dividing them based on fallacies and misunderstandings.

Wintley Phipps, who has sung for US presidents and other world leaders including South African president Nelson Mandela, understands the importance of correcting this wrong. As a native of Trinidad and Tobago, as a former resident of Canada, as an American citizen, and as a man of African descent, Phipps speaks with passion about the issue of the Christian faith and its often-misunderstood connection to people of color.

Phipps narrates a fascinating journey for truth throughout this study—with much of it based in Africa itself—specifically in Egypt, Sudan, and other areas that surround the Nile River region. Along the way, experts such as Dr. Edwin Yamauchi, Dr. Allen Callahan, Dr. Catherine Kroeger, Dr. Roland Werner—and laypeople with a heart for discovery, such as soccer star Desmond Armstrong and businessman Dana Gonsal, add texture to the search for truth.

As the study proceeds, several vital truths are established—and primary among them is the clear truth that a misinterpreted Scripture verse in the book of Genesis does not mean that any group of people—especially the people who descended from Noah's son Ham—are cursed to a life of servitude and inferiority. Indeed, as Phipps clearly points out, all people who know Jesus, regardless of their ethnicity, are one in Christ with equal standing before God and in the human community.

It is refreshing to examine this and other vital realities—such as the implications of Philip's encounter with the official from Ethiopia and the Old Testament references to people from Africa. And it is encouraging to see fellow believers in Jesus Christ freed from the burdens of historical misconceptions so they can live openly with a new understanding of both their own heritage and their personal faith in Jesus.

Take the journey with these friends as they help us see the breadth and depth of the Christian experience—no matter what our background.

—Dave Branon
Editor

The Myth of a Cursed Race

DAYLIGHT PREVIEW

A Legacy of Shame

How could it be that one Bible verse—so misinterpreted and so misapplied—could have had such a devastating and destructive effect on so many people? Noah's curse of his grandson Canaan, found in Genesis 9:25, has caused unspeakable heartbreak, cruelty, and disgrace for a race of people it does not even mention. In this session, Wintley Phipps explains how the misuse of this verse has touched his ancestors and all who were subjected to mistreatment that was never intended by Noah. Carefully researched and clearly explained, the so-called "Curse of Ham" is addressed—too late for the millions who have been damaged by it but not too late to help us all understand a little better the great contributions Africans have made to both society and the Christian church.

——————— COME TOGETHER ———————
Icebreaker Questions

1. As Wintley Phipps notes, each of us is initially identified by our name. What's the story behind how you were given your first name?

2. This series features maps and discussions about where locations in antiquity can be found today. What's your favorite way to get directions to a

new place? When was the last time you used an old-fashioned, printed map?

3. How racially diverse was the community where you grew up? How racially diverse is the community you live in now?

FINDING DAYLIGHT

Experience the Video

Feel free to jot down Video Notes as you watch the presentation by Wintley Phipps. Use the space below for those notes.

———————————————VIDEO NOTES———————————————

A question of identity

A motherless child

The effects of slavery

A question of heritage

Equal before God

Tragic misuse of God's Word

Dr. Edwin Yamauchi

The curse: Canaan, not Ham

The curse fulfilled: Hebrews conquer Canaan

Mizraim, Put, Cush: In Africa

Dr. Roland Werner

Dr. Allen Callahan

Development of the curse

Slavery

WALKING IN THE DAYLIGHT

Discussion Time

———————————DISCOVER GOD'S WORD———————————
Discussion/Application Questions

1. In introducing the topic of the slavery of black Africans, Wintley
    Phipps says, "Just imagine being captured and treated like animals,
    being shipped away forever from your family and your home. Imag-
    ine being sold like cattle. Imagine losing your language—and yes,
    even your name."

    What emotions rise within you when you think about what these peo-
    ple were forced to endure?

2. As Dr. Edwin Yamauchi says, if there's one verse in the Bible that has
    adversely affected Africans, it's Genesis 9:25. Take a look at that
    verse in its context by reading Genesis 9:18–27.

    What do you think Ham did wrong?

3. This Scripture passage is the basis of the so-called "curse of Ham." But upon whom did Noah actually pronounce a curse?

4. When Joshua led the Israelites (who were "Semites"—descendants of Noah's son Shem) into Canaan, the Promised Land, they would personally experience the sinfulness of the Canaanites (Leviticus 18) and the severity of God's judgment upon them. The Canaanites would become "the lowest of slaves" (Genesis 9:25) by being subjugated to the Israelites (Joshua 9:27; 16:10; Judges 1:27–35).

    a. Why is it important to remember that Genesis was primarily written for and addressed to Israel? How could that affect the emphasis on Canaan in Genesis 9?

    b. In light of the concept that the "curse of Ham" supposedly consigned black Africans to being both dark-skinned and enslaved, what is the significance of the fact that most of Ham's descendants—including the Canaanites—were Caucasians?

5. Some people—for example, some ancient Jews—tried to extend the curse of Ham to Ham's other sons, particularly to his son Cush (see Genesis 10:6), who settled in a region that came to be called by the same name, located south of Egypt in modern Sudan.

    In terms of the text of Genesis 9, how logical is this notion that the curse of Ham resulted in the descendants of Cush being marked by black skin and inferior worth?

6. According to Dr. Yamauchi, Muslims then used this curse, evidently in a garbled tradition, to say that black Africans were doubly cursed: They were black because of the curse, and they were destined to be slaves because of the curse.

    How would that serve as a convenient justification for Muslims, who had a long history of enslaving black Africans?

7. The curse of Ham also appears among European writers and was strongly used by pro-slave advocates in the United States before the Civil War.

    How do you suppose white Christians in Europe and America were able to convince themselves that Genesis 9 endorses the enslavement of black Africans?

──────────────── BRINGING IT HOME ────────────────

1. How do you feel about talking about issues related to race?

2. Wintley states that although the earliest use of the curse of Ham to justify slavery in America dates back to the 1670s, the effect of that teaching is still felt today.

    How do you think the effect of that teaching is still being felt today in our society? In your specific circles?

3. What do you hope to gain from this study and from spending time with this group?

DAYLIGHT ON PRAYER

Spending Time with God

1. How can the group pray for you as you begin this study?

2. Do you have any other prayer requests you'd like to share with the group?

As you pray together, be encouraged by these words from Wintley Phipps:

> "Many of African and slave descent have wondered at some point in their lives about their heritage and their identity. They have wondered about who they really are. But for those of us who take the Bible seriously, we know that no matter the race, the color, or ethnicity, we are all God's children. We know that in the eyes of God we are all equal and that no one is cursed because of color or race."

DAYLIGHT AHEAD

A pilgrimage is in store as you head into Session 2. Join a group of people on a study tour of Africa as they explore, with the help of Dr. Catherine Kroeger, a number of sites that depict the influence of ancient Africans in lands around the Nile River. Along the way, you'll also learn about some specific references in Scripture to African leaders who were part of Old Testament stories.

A Convenient Lie

DAYLIGHT PREVIEW

A Visit To Africa

Sadly, a single, misinterpreted verse in the Old Testament has contributed to untold pain and suffering for an entire race of people made in God's image. To help us get a fresh perspective on the value and the contribution of this people group, travel with Dr. Catherine Kroeger as she guides a pilgrimage back to Africa and back to the pages of the Bible.

──────── COME TOGETHER ────────
Icebreaker Questions

1. This session begins with Wintley Phipps making a reference to "cheap labor." Do you remember how much you made per hour in your first job?

2. Have you ever made a pilgrimage to where your ancestors used to live? If so, what was it like? If not, how eager are you to do so?

3. Dr. Catherine Kroeger was an enthusiastic professor who continued leading study tours to Africa in her eighties. What would you love to do when you're in your eighties? (Note: Dr. Kroeger died in 2011 at the age of 85.)

FINDING DAYLIGHT

Experience the Video

Feel free to jot down Video Notes as you watch the presentation by Wintley Phipps. Use the space below for those notes.

──────────────── VIDEO NOTES ────────────────

Slaves and cheap labor

God's love

A pilgrimage back to Africa

Lessette: A search for truth

Leroy Attles: Appreciate God's creation

Utibe: The curse

Dr. Catherine Kroeger

Culture along the Nile

Black Pharaoh: Tirhakah

Tirhakah rescues the Hebrews

The Bible and Cush

    Moses

    Jeremiah

    Ethiopian eunuch

No one is excluded

WALKING IN THE DAYLIGHT

Discussion Time

────────── DISCOVER GOD'S WORD ──────────
Discussion/Application Questions

1. **Wintley Phipps doesn't pull any punches as he begins this session by saying that an isolated verse in the book of Genesis became a convenient lie and a rationalization for greed, since the truth was that using slaves meant cheap labor.**

   How do you think slave owners who professed to be Christians yet believed that the black race was cursed to be slaves dealt with what Wintley calls the central teaching of the Bible—God's love for the whole world, which is expressed in John 3:16: "For God so loved the world that He gave His one and only Son, that whoever believes in Him shall not perish but have eternal life"?

2. **This session follows a group of students participating in the Africa and the Bible study tour in Africa.**

   a. What are the benefits for an African-American Christian going on a pilgrimage to Africa? Can you see any risks in such an endeavor?

   b. How would you compare this kind of pilgrimage with ones taken by other people who visit the land where their ancestors used to live?

3. A Cushite named Shabako gained control of Egypt in 715 BC, founding the 25th Dynasty. Egypt continued to be ruled by this Cushite dynasty until 663 BC. Both 2 Kings 19:9 and Isaiah 37:9 recount how King Sennacherib of Assyria was threatening Judah but then received a report that Tirhakah, the Cushite king of Egypt, was marching out to fight against him. By coming to Judah's aid, Tirhakah helped spare Judah from the Assyrians, at least for the time being.

   a. How do you respond to discovering that Tirhakah, one of the pharaohs of Egypt, was black? What significance do you see in that fact?

   b. What do you think Rev. Mark Fowler, a participant in the study tour, means when he says, "It matters not to me if the pharaoh was black. What matters to me is that the truth be brought forth"?

4. Dr. Edwin Yamauchi points out Scripture passages in which he believes black Africans are mentioned, such as Moses' Cushite wife (Numbers 12:1), a Cushite named Ebed-Melech who saved Jeremiah's life (Jeremiah 38:7–13), and the eunuch from Ethiopia (Acts 8:26–40).

   How should we balance that reality with Dr. Yamauchi's statement that "a basic principle is that it is not necessary for one to find one's ethnic group mentioned in the Bible in order to accept the biblical message for oneself"?

5. **Isaiah 18:1-7 represents a prophecy against Cush. Read verses 1–2.**

   Cush was located just south of Egypt, in modern Sudan. In ancient times it was also known as Nubia or Ethiopia (not to be confused with modern Ethiopia, which is farther southeast). The "whirring wings" in verse 1 could refer either literally to insects, for which the Nile valley was notorious, or figuratively to the armies of Cush. Chapters 18–20 of Isaiah address Egypt and Cush, which were united at this time.

   How does Isaiah describe the people of Cush?

6. **Evidently the Cushite king had sent envoys to Hezekiah, the king of Judah, no doubt to try to persuade Judah to join Cush and Egypt in a coalition against the Assyrians. The Lord inspired the prophet Isaiah to urge the ambassadors to return home with the message recorded in verses 3–6. All the nations of the world—not just the threatening Assyrians but nations such as Cush and Egypt—are condemned for their hostility.**

   Now read verse 7.

   a. In what way is this consistent with the language of verses 1–2?

   b. On the other hand, how does this represent a major shift in tone from the previous words of judgment?

7. Surely verse 7 looks beyond the impending defeat of Cush and Egypt at the hands of the Assyrians.

   What is God's ultimate desire for an aggressive nation like Cush?

8. Throughout the Bible, we see that God's final plan is to gather a worshiping people from all nations. Catch a glimpse of that plan by reading what God showed the apostle John in Revelation 5:1–10.

   What does this heavenly scene, with its exalted images of Jesus Christ, say to the concept of the so-called "curse of Ham" and the erroneous idea of the inferior race that was spawned as a result?

BRINGING IT HOME

In reference to the Africa and the Bible study tour, Rev. Leroy Attles says, "What we want to do is appreciate all of God's creation. And it's hard to appreciate God's creation if you yourself feel that you are an inferior part of God's creation."

How much of a challenge has that been for you?

DAYLIGHT ON PRAYER

Spending Time with God

1. What prayer requests would you like to share with the group?

2. Wintley Phipps closes this session by saying, "All people everywhere are invited to be a part of God's family and God's kingdom. No one is excluded. No one is cursed because of some shade of color or one's appearance or because they are a man or a woman. For God sees nothing but our hearts. And when our hearts are His, we are all one in Christ. Jesus loved you all the way to the cross. And He's coming back again for men and women from every race, nation, kindred, tongue, and people."

Conclude your prayer time by thanking God for His inclusive love and for His marvelous plan to bring all kinds of people together through His Son Jesus.

DAYLIGHT AHEAD

You'll put a face to the questions that trouble many men and women of African heritage as former world-class soccer star for the United States, Desmond Armstrong, takes a personal journey to examine the connections between Africa and the Bible. These are connections that help Desmond as he helps his own children understand the value of Christianity in their lives.

White Man's Religion?

DAYLIGHT PREVIEW

Roots

One of the battles people of African descent have to face as they approach Christianity is the reputation that this faith is a "white man's religion." One American who has done a lot of research into this topic to find out if this is true is Desmond Armstrong. A 2012 inductee into the US National Soccer Hall of Fame and a father of six children, Armstrong has examined Scripture and has studied under the tutelage of Dr. Catherine Kroeger to learn how people of his race can relate more readily to Christianity.

COME TOGETHER

Icebreaker Questions

1. Wintley Phipps begins this session by talking about the beloved spirituals that arose out of slavery. What songs stand out in your childhood memories?

2. The students in Dr. Kroeger's class raved about how much they learned. What class or teacher stands out in your memory in that way?

3. What class or field of study do you wish you could take now?

FINDING DAYLIGHT

Experience the Video

Feel free to jot down Video Notes as you watch the presentation by Wintley Phipps. Use the space below for those notes.

──────────────── VIDEO NOTES ────────────────

A stained past

Spirituals

Desmond Armstrong

Africa and the Bible

Dr. Kroeger's class

Handshake with an African brother

Desmond's Q and A

Desmond and Dr. Kroeger

Roots: Spiritual and physical

The study tour

Truth

WALKING IN THE DAYLIGHT

Discussion Time

---------------------DISCOVER GOD'S WORD---------------------
Discussion/Application Questions

1. How would you respond to someone who still contends that Christianity is the white man's religion?

2. Why would the spirituals, the slaves' musical expression of faith, represent "a disturbing kind of joy" for converted slaves?

3. Why is it important for African-American Christians to realize, as Desmond Armstrong says, that the roots of their faith "didn't just start here on the shores of America—it started way back in Africa"?

4. Dr. Kroeger shared about Quodvultdeus, an influential bishop of Carthage, in North Africa.

What significance does the existence of this black bishop from the fifth century have for African-American Christians today?

5. Why do you think African-Americans, especially young black men, are so attracted to Islam?

6. How can Christians, particularly African-American Christians, counteract that attraction?

7. What can believers—both African-American and Caucasian—do now to try to bring healing and reconciliation in light of the stained past of slavery?

8. Dr. Kroeger lived in the same house in which several generations of her family were conceived, born, and died. And she said she longed for African-American people to experience a similar strong sense of history.

    a. How realistic is that hope?

    b. What did Dr. Kroeger mean when she said we also need to understand our spiritual roots and claim that faith?

    c. Can someone who doesn't have Christian family roots still do that?

—————————— BRINGING IT HOME ——————————

1. Dr. Kroeger invited Desmond to her home on Cape Cod, where they discussed their roots. She contended that all of us need to know our roots—where we came from.

    a. How much do you know about your family's roots, particularly in terms of a spiritual legacy?

b. What are some additional things you wish you could discover about your heritage?

2. Dr. Kroeger wasn't content simply to teach classes about Africa and great Africans in the Bible. She explained that she was leading a study tour to Africa "to instill in persons of African descent a sense of confidence in God's love for them, in God's empowerment for them, in God's place of importance for them."

Regardless of your racial and cultural background, how high is your level of confidence in God's love for you, in God's empowerment for you, and in God's place of importance for you?

 DAYLIGHT ON PRAYER

Spending Time with God

1. Spend time interceding in regard to some of the areas touched on in this session:

   • for African-Americans, especially young black men, to be attracted to Jesus and Christianity rather than Islam
   • for healing and reconciliation in light of the stained past of slavery
   • for African-Americans to experience a strong sense of history—and in a way that would provide confidence in God's love for them, in God's empowerment for them, and in God's place of importance for them

2. What personal concerns would you like the group to pray with you about?

 DAYLIGHT AHEAD

A group of Ethiopian Christians walks through the streets of Jerusalem to reenact the triumphal entry of Jesus into Jerusalem. Why is this important? Think about the story of Philip in Acts 8—the story of his encounter with an official from Ethiopia—and you just might begin to see how these worshipers connect their current faith to the heritage of this man whose story is found in the New Testament.

What Is Truth?

DAYLIGHT PREVIEW

Taking the Truth to Africa

Most Christians who have studied the Bible at all are familiar with the story in Acts 8 of Philip's being led by the Holy Spirit to a desert road that ran from Jerusalem to Gaza (which is on the west side of Israel near the Mediterranean Sea). Rarely do readers consider, however, the cultural implications. The person Philip was led to was an official of a queen from the African nation of Meroe. Therefore, this official, one of the early converts to Christianity, was a dark-skinned citizen of an African country—and he took this new faith with him to his homeland. In his excitement, we can assume, he would have shared the gospel with others in Meroe, which is now Sudan.

COME TOGETHER

Icebreaker Questions

1. This session begins with the oldest known manuscript fragment of the New Testament, which is written on papyrus paper. Do you prefer to read from paper or on electronic devices? What percentage of your reading would you guess to be from paper and what percentage would you guess to be on electronic devices?

2. Dr. Edwin Yamauchi notes that the term *Ethiopia* comes from a Greek word that means "sunburned face." What's the worst sunburn you can remember?

3. This session focuses on a story in Acts about a royal treasurer. Has anyone in the group ever served as the treasurer of an organization or club? How did that go?

 # FINDING DAYLIGHT

Experience the Video

Feel free to jot down Video Notes as you watch the presentation by Wintley Phipps. Use the space below for those notes.

—————————— VIDEO NOTES ——————————

Jesus' message reaches Egypt

Ethiopia and Christianity

The eunuch and Ethiopia

Royal treasurer: Acts 8

The gospel goes to Ethiopia

Meroe in Africa: Everybody's religion

Europeans and Africans

Desmond on Jesus

The land of Jesus: A crossroads

WALKING IN THE DAYLIGHT

Discussion Time

——————————— DISCOVER GOD'S WORD ———————————

Discussion/Application Questions

1. The oldest known manuscript fragment of the New Testament is a
    small section of John 18. Dated most likely to the first half of the
    second century, this piece of papyrus paper was discovered in Egypt

·

and is now housed in the John Rylands Library at the University of Manchester in England.

How does this ancient record of Jesus' trial before Pilate stand as evidence not only of the truth about Jesus the King but also of the reality that the story of Jesus had reached Africa just a few decades after the apostle John originally wrote his gospel?

2. In the video we see some Ethiopian Orthodox Christians celebrating Palm Sunday in Jerusalem. These Orthodox Christians trace their spiritual beginnings back to one man. Read about him in Acts 8:26–40.

As Dr. Edwin Yamauchi and Dr. Roland Werner point out, this official wasn't from modern Ethiopia but from the kingdom of Meroe, which today is part of the country of the Sudan. Meroe was ruled by a queen mother who had the dynastic title of Candace and who ruled on behalf of her son. He was the king, but he was viewed as too sacred to participate in the secular functions of the government because he was considered the child of the sun.

The fact that this important minister of finance—despite being a Gentile—had gone to Jerusalem to worship shows that he was either a full-fledged Jewish proselyte or at least a "God-fearer"—one who was attracted to Judaism.

How does Luke, the author of Acts, emphasize that this encounter was clearly orchestrated by God?

3. While in Jerusalem, the official had evidently purchased a copy of the book of Isaiah—likely in Greek, which was used as a court language in the kingdom of Meroe at the time.

Why was the particular passage the official was reading, Isaiah 53:7–8, ideal for Philip to use as a starting point to explain to him the good news about Jesus?

4. Although we don't know what happened to this man afterwards, verse 39 says that he went on his way rejoicing—likely all the way back to Sudan. One early church father, Irenaeus, wrote that the official became a missionary to the Ethiopians. Dr. Kroeger states that the church fathers were excited that the gospel had gone deep into Africa and that it had been taken by a dark-skinned person.

Why does the fact that the gospel advanced to Africa by an African make this development even more exciting?

5. What does Dr. Allen Callahan mean when he says that the apostle Paul becomes sort of the poster child of European Christianity?

6. What do you think of the notion that the church has been quite Eurocentric for much of the last two thousand years, which has led African-Americans to view Christianity as the white man's religion and to be attracted to Islam instead?

7. How do you tend to view Jesus' physical appearance in your mind's eye?

8. How do you feel about Desmond Armstrong's first point that Jesus came from a land in which the people are dark-hued, and therefore Jesus was definitely not blond-haired and blue-eyed?

9. How do you feel about Desmond's second point that Scripture itself doesn't give a physical description of Jesus for a good reason—i.e., we need to focus on what Christ did and said and how to apply His Word to our individual lives, rather than becoming so fixated on His physical appearance that it becomes an icon or an idol for us?

——————————— BRINGING IT HOME ———————————

Philip and the Ethiopian eunuch clearly had a "divine appointment."

a. What people or events has God used to draw you to a relationship with Jesus?

b. Can you recall being part of a divine appointment, either from the side of Philip (sharing the message) or the Ethiopian (hearing the message)?

c. How willing would you be to take advantage of the kind of situation that God gave Philip?

DAYLIGHT ON PRAYER

Spending Time with God

1. What concerns for yourself, others, or world events would you like the group to pray with you about?

2. In Galatians 3:28, the apostle Paul declares, "There is neither Jew nor Greek, slave nor free, male nor female, for you are all one in Christ Jesus."

    Conclude your prayer time by thanking God that Christianity is everybody's religion.

DAYLIGHT AHEAD

An exciting mystery begins to be solved as researchers examine the connections between Christianity and the peoples of Africa. It becomes increasingly clear that the gospel took hold in the northeast corner of Africa long before it made its way to Europe and beyond. A visit to Cairo and a trip down the Nile River reveal exciting news about men and women who share a heritage of faith in Christ that goes back to the beginnings of Christianity.

The River of Faith

DAYLIGHT PREVIEW

Connections to the Nile

Men like Dana Gonsal have long wondered how people of African descent could ever embrace Christianity. After all, during the terrible time of slavery in America and Europe, the proponents of the practice often professed to be Christians. But then Gonsal, a Boston businessman who created his own company by hard work and determination, began to research the early church fathers who dealt with the selection of the canon—the books of Scripture. They, he discovered, were from North Africa. Others who studied the early church found out that cities all up and down the Nile River had connections to the gospel from its earliest days. Clearly, Christianity is not a European religion for white people—but a universal truth for all.

COME TOGETHER

Icebreaker Questions

1. After arriving in Egypt on an overnight trans-Atlantic flight, Dr. Catherine Kroeger immediately took her students to church. How much trouble have you had with jet lag after a long flight?

2. The church that the students went to was unique—meeting in a cave, for one thing. Can you think of an unusual church you have visited? What church would you like to visit?

3. Alexandria's giant lighthouse was one of the seven wonders of the ancient world. Have you visited any noteworthy lighthouses?

 # FINDING DAYLIGHT

Experience the Video

Feel free to jot down Video Notes as you watch the presentation by Wintley Phipps. Use the space below for those notes.

————————————VIDEO NOTES————————————

Dr. Kroeger's hope

The cave church

Garbage collectors

Africa's early access to Christianity

Alexandria: Christian light

Dana Gonsal: Why embrace Christianity?

Great African Christian kingdom

WALKING IN THE DAYLIGHT

Discussion Time

———————————DISCOVER GOD'S WORD———————————
Discussion/Application Questions

1. Wintley Phipps begins this session by stating that for many people of
    African descent, as descendants of slaves, chains are a reminder of
    a less than Christian past, and the faith of the cross is viewed as the
    faith of slavery—the faith of suffering.

    How does the information presented in this study about the history of
    Christianity in Africa speak to that perception?

2. How do you think you would be affected by visiting the Arab wor-
    shipers at their large cave church in Cairo at night and then return-
    ing the next day to find these same people searching and sorting
    through trash?

3. Why did some of the students feel a special bond of fellowship with the garbage collectors who comprise that church?

4. Wintley notes that Alexandria had a giant lighthouse that was one of the seven wonders of the ancient Greek world, and the light of the Christian faith began to shine from this region—light that helped change even the Roman Empire.

   How does the large cave in Cairo represent light and hope now to the garbage collectors who go to church there?

5. How surprised were you to learn that people in Africa became followers of Christ long before Christianity was preached to the Germans or English or any other northern European tribes and nations?

6. In this session we meet Dana Gonsal, whose own life was changed as he discovered the faith of his African fathers.

   a. Why do you think the fact that Jesus had a Jewish background made it even harder for Dana to embrace Him and Christianity?

b. Why do you think the fact that so many leaders and bishops in the early church—such as Tertullian, Origen, Augustine, Athanasius, and Cyprian—came from Africa changed his life?

7. **Though these leaders came from North Africa, a great African Christian kingdom clearly arose farther to the south, in modern Sudan.**

How do you imagine European travelers in the eleventh and the twelfth centuries felt when they met Nubian monks and believers who—with their dark faces, and some of them with the sign of the cross branded on their foreheads—were on a pilgrimage to Jerusalem?

────── BRINGING IT HOME ──────

Dana Gonsal's passion is to tell everybody he can that all Christians—regardless of race or gender—are important and have a contribution to make.

a. How strongly do you share that conviction?

b. What is *your* spiritual passion?

DAYLIGHT ON PRAYER

Spending Time with God

1. Pray for each other based on what was just shared. Ask God to place His passion within you and to produce fruit in that regard.

2. What other prayer requests would you like to share with the group?

DAYLIGHT AHEAD

A trip five hundred miles down the Nile takes pilgrims to Aswan, a city that leads to the ancient kingdom of Nubia. There, it was discovered, stood a long history of a Christian community that existed for a thousand years in this land. Archaeological findings reveal pictures and other evidence that Nubians believed in all the main tenets of Christianity. These African people clearly lived out the Christian life based on Jesus' victory and God's Word.

Discoveries at Aswan

DAYLIGHT PREVIEW

A Rich History

A trip into Africa via the Nile River renewed for a group of people on a study tour the reality that there does not have to be a stigma attached to Christianity that is based on race. One of the pilgrims stated that all of the races "play a part in the body of Christ." They saw fellow believers who work in garbage dumps in Cairo, and they saw that the kingdom of Nubia honored Jesus through art and worship. They saw clearly that the gospel of Jesus Christ is not the possession of any one group—but that it is the gospel of all peoples. What a difference this could make for today's church if all believers were to embrace this truth.

COME TOGETHER

Icebreaker Questions

1. Much of this session takes place along the Nile River. What special memories do you have of spending time on or by a river?

2. In Aswan, boats with triangle sails glide upstream and downstream as they have for centuries. Have you done much sailing? Do you have any good sailing stories?

3. The Nubian people of Aswan value hospitality highly. What fond memories of hospitality do you have from your childhood?

FINDING DAYLIGHT

Experience the Video

Feel free to jot down Video Notes as you watch the presentation by Wintley Phipps. Use the space below for those notes.

──────────────── VIDEO NOTES ────────────────

Journey to Aswan

Nubians

    Homes

    Faith

Nubian Christian kingdom

    Discovery of surprising pieces of art

c. 530–1400s

Emphasis on the cross

Temples into churches

Nubian manuscript

The Christian faith was lost

Remnants of Christianity

Cairo Christian church

Roots of Christianity for Africans, before slavery

Salvation is offered to all

WALKING IN THE DAYLIGHT

Discussion Time

———————————— DISCOVER GOD'S WORD ————————————
Discussion/Application Questions

1. This session focuses on the Nubian Christian kingdom that existed for almost a thousand years, from the 500s until the 1400s. Dr. Roland Werner states that these Christians believed in the basic teachings of the Bible but were especially intrigued with the cross, not so much as a sign of Christ's passion but more as a symbol of His victory over sin and the devil and the world.

    Can you think of some Scriptures that support that emphasis?

2. Inside the pagan temple of Philae at Aswan, a cross carved into the stone marks the conversion of this temple. An inscription reads, "The cross has won. It always wins!"

    How would our individual lives, our churches, and our nation be different if we, like the ancient Nubian Christians, experienced a surge of admiration for the glory and power of the cross?

3. Wintley Phipps states, "After almost a thousand years the faith of the cross was eventually conquered—conquered partly from within, because the Nubians had begun to trust in the kingdom of man, to trust the political power of their Christian kingdom rather than God. The words of Christ were forgotten. There was no one left to wield the Christian weapons of faith and truth. And so, over time,

conquest by those carrying the Muslim crescent brought not only a loss of freedom but also full surrender of the cross."

Do you see a warning here for Christians today? If so, what is the appropriate response?

4. Dr. Werner notes that traces of Christianity can still be found in the Sudan. Babies are taken to the Nile to be "baptized with the baptism of John." And when a child is ill, oil or butter or flour is used to make the sign of the cross on the child's belly in order to ward off evil spirits or sickness. But the knowledge of what all of this really means has been lost.

Again, do you see a warning here for Christians today? And if so, what is the appropriate response?

5. Vince, one of the study tour participants, states, "I can say, 'I'm black and I'm proud.' And others can say, 'I'm white and I'm proud,' or 'I'm Hispanic and I'm proud,' or 'I'm Asian and I'm proud.' And rather than being divisive, we are celebrating these differences."

Do you agree with Vince that this is a healthy kind of pride—pride in the way God has made us? Or do you see it as an unhealthy attitude of ethnocentrism?

6. Just before their flight home, the study group visited an Arab-speaking Christian church in the center of Cairo. As Wintley says, even though language may be a barrier with these worshipers, the Spirit of Christ makes them one.

a. Have you ever been part of a church or Christian organization in which there were potential barriers such as different languages, races, or cultures? If so, how did that go?

b. In your opinion, what is the key to the success of a church or organization that is heterogeneous, or integrated, rather than homogenous?

7. **Many Christian leaders who study church growth and help churches grow affirm people's inclination to worship and fellowship with others of their own race and background. Other Christian voices have denounced that approach as falling short of God's desire for unity in diversity—and that it may even promote segregation and prejudice.**

How do you think believers should respond to this issue in a way that pleases the Lord and advances His kingdom?

BRINGING IT HOME

1. **"The cross has won. It always wins!"**

a. What does that mean to you?

b. In what area of your life does the cross need to win or gain more ground?

2. **What have you appreciated the most about this study and about this group?**

DAYLIGHT ON PRAYER

Spending Time with God

1. How can the group pray for you in regard to your ongoing walk with Christ?

2. Wintley Phipps concludes this study by saying, "My prayer is that Christian descendants of those slaves will now rest on the river of our ancient faith and become a collective voice of reconciliation, proving once again that the salvation provided through the glorious cross of Jesus Christ is offered to people of all races and all nations."

Conclude by asking the Lord to bring that prayer to fulfillment.